15 EASY WAYS TO OVERCOME WRITER'S BLOCK

AND START WRITING TODAY

Natalya Androsova, PhD

North Spirit Publishers
Toronto, Canada

Copyright © 2023 Natalya Androsova

All rights reserved. No part of this book may be reproduced, distributed, or used in any form or by any means, including photocopying, recording, or other electronic or mechanical methods, without the prior written permission of the publisher, except for the use of brief quotations embedded in critical reviews.

Editing by Amber Lambda
Cover by Olayemi Bolaji
Book design by Eswari Kamireddy

978-1-7774537-5-6 (Paperback)
978-1-7774537-6-3 (E-book)

Also by Natalya Androsova

Dissertation Without Tears: How to Break Up with Your Inner Critic and Nourish the Writer Within

7 Minutes to Freedom: Simple Writing Meditations to Liberate Your Writing and Your Life

The Gratitude Effect
Co-Author with Dr. John Demartini

Meet Natalya at
www.writingdissertationcoach.com

For every writer tied down by writer's block:

May today be the day you break free and fly!

Acknowledgements

I am grateful to

Richard, for being patient and encouraging me to follow my dreams

Angela Joosse, for being compassionate and gracious

Anastasia Lakhtikova, for being passionate and direct

Amber Lambda, for being clear and creative

Christina, Ingrid, Angela, Diane, Andrea, and Annie, for being supportive and kind

My coaching clients, for being inspiring and brave

Contents

Introduction 1
How to Use This Book 3

Part 1: I Can't Start! 7

I've been stuck for too long. It will take me
forever to get back into my writing flow. 9
I feel too much pressure. 15
I feel overwhelmed by how much I have to do. 21
I can't start until I know how it's all going to fit together. 27
I don't know where to start. 33
I have too many things to do before I can start writing. ... 39
I hate writing! 45

Part 2: I Can't Continue! 51

I'm stuck in this section and can't
move on until I figure it out. 53
I've rewritten this section five times,
but can't move on until it's polished. 59
I'm going in circles. I don't know what to say. 65
I'm afraid of being wrong. 71
Nothing is going to plan! Might as well give up. 77
I'm too tired to continue writing. 83
I don't feel like writing today. Or ever. I quit! 89
What I'm undertaking feels impossible.
I feel too discouraged to continue. 95

A Note from the Author 101

Introduction

*I*f you've ever experienced writer's block, then you know the excruciating pain of being stuck—not knowing where to start or go next, not finding the right words, and losing your sense of purpose.

I've been there in that pain, stress, and overwhelm. I felt a sense of being lost and going in circles. Frustrated, discouraged, unable to figure it out and ready to quit. Not knowing how and if it's all going to fit together. I felt like nothing was going to plan, and the loud cries of self-doubt and my inner critic were the only voices in my head!

No one is immune to these voices. In fact, it's a normal part of the writing process. The real danger is that a small writer's block has the potential to grow bigger and bigger, keeping a writer stuck for a long time. This is a very painful feeling—to see a writer without hope or direction for weeks or even months. But it's unnecessary to stay in that dark place for as long as we do.

Yes, the writing momentum is precious, but it's important to know that if you've lost it, it's only a temporary change. Don't give this little stumble too much importance. Writing momentum is transient. It comes and goes, and it's okay.

Having helped hundreds of writers to overcome writer's block, I want to assure you that it is nothing to fear. You can beat it. Fast! And you can jump right back into the flow. I want to show you how because I have witnessed this time and again in myself and others. You can reset and start writing in a matter of hours or even minutes.

I know it doesn't feel this way when you are the one who is stuck. Therefore, I've collected my best, proven, and reliable tools, tips, and strategies into this handbook. My intention is to help you overcome writer's block and go back to your writing as soon as possible.

My other intention is to create a safe place for you to come to when you're feeling stuck, stressed, and overwhelmed. I hope you allow yourself to feel what you're feeling, pick up this book for a few minutes, be inspired, reset, and gather all your strength to get back into the game!

I hope you know how brave you are to be sharing yourself with the world, how strong, open, and vulnerable you are to face the blank page, and how precious your time with your writing is. Enjoy every moment, and treat yourself and your writing with the kindness and respect you both deserve!

This is my intention and offer. Do I have your commitment to try?

How to Use This Book

This is not a cover to cover read. This is a handbook organized to be helpful to you in the present moment. My goal is simple—to get you from reading my words to writing yours in minutes!

I've identified 15 specific thoughts that cause writer's block and named each chapter after one. So whenever you feel stuck, you can scan through the table of contents, find the culprit thought, flip to that section in the book, and focus on the block you're struggling with. The whole point is to deal with the block right there and then.

Each section defines the problem and offers healthy solutions, including a list of creative and practical ideas for you to experiment with until you find what works for YOU. Finally, you can play with 4-5 freewriting prompts designed to help with that specific block and to jumpstart your writing.

I'm happy to share the tips and tricks that have helped me and so many of my students. My hope is that they will help you return to your writing flow quickly. These are simple and effective tools, but only if you try them. If you don't apply them, they will not work. Getting more information is a sophisticated procrastination technique. But your commitment to changing your writing experience will create miracles!

Are you ready to say goodbye to writer's block once and for all? You can do it! I believe in you!

There is no greater agony than bearing an untold story inside you.
— Maya Angelou

PART 1
I CAN'T START!

Start writing, no matter what. The water does not flow until the faucet is turned on.
— Louis L'Amour

I'VE BEEN STUCK FOR TOO LONG. IT WILL TAKE ME FOREVER TO GET BACK INTO MY WRITING FLOW.

PROBLEM

> You haven't built enough trust in your writing practice.

As a coach, one of the greatest misconceptions about writing I see is a belief that it takes a long time to get rid of stress and overwhelm and achieve the flow. After you've been struggling with writing for weeks or months, you might develop a belief that change will also take weeks or months. It's completely understandable. It's been too painful for too long. But it's not a reason to give up.

SOLUTION

> Allow yourself to start over and develop a healthy practice.

Working with hundreds of writers, I've seen time and again that it doesn't take weeks or months to change your practice. A change happens in one moment. One moment of clarity and insight. It might take a couple of weeks to fully integrate that clarity and insight into your routine, but right away, you will feel the emotional relief from the pressure you used to put on yourself and your writing.

It takes no time for clarity, momentum, and joy to replace stress and overwhelm. I've seen hundreds of breakthroughs happen effortlessly in the moment of openness, readiness, and a strong commitment to change your process.

So please know that you're not stuck in a painful writing stage forever. You're one moment away from a powerful and lasting change. You are about to build a healthy, sustainable, and joyful practice that works so well that you can't wait to run to your desk!

The first thing I'm going to ask you to do is to stop pushing yourself. Slow down and allow yourself to pause and to breathe. You are doing something very important. You are building a radically new practice to enjoy for the rest of your life. Take your time.

Let's put down all your grandiose goals and set a new and modest one. For the next five days, your only goal is to come to your writing, gently touch it, and spend some time with it every day. Where do you want to start? 15 minutes a day? 30 minutes? An hour? What feels possible and exciting? Start small and spend some time with your project and your process. What are you noticing? Please journal through this process. And promise me that on days six and seven you will take a break! Promise? Okay. I trust you!

This is the single most powerful writing secret—building a reliable, healthy, and joyful daily routine! This is it. Once you try it, you will see the benefits for yourself and will never go back. Your trust in your process and your relationship with your writing will change forever. I'm excited for the rest of your writing life from this moment on!

PRACTICAL IDEAS TO TRY

Enjoy playing with these creative ideas to jumpstart your session!

- Create a writing schedule for the next five days. Schedule a 15-45 minute session and write it down in your calendar, so you know exactly when you will be writing every day. Schedule something fun for days six and seven. Repeat next week.

- Set your alarm for five minutes and freewrite about anything that comes to mind in response to what you're currently researching or writing about—insights, questions, comments, ideas, or possible directions.

- Imagine what it would feel like to write consistently every day, be productive, feel motivated, and enjoy your work. Freewrite for five minutes as if you're already there. What do you feel?

PROMPTS

Finish the sentences below as quickly as you can, and as many times as you want. Afterwards, freewrite for five minutes about any responses that surprised you.

If I knew I couldn't fail, I would write about…
………………………………………………………………………………
………………………………………………………………………………

What feels inauthentic at the moment is…
………………………………………………………………………………
………………………………………………………………………………

I feel what got me stuck is…
………………………………………………………………………………
………………………………………………………………………………

What's really causing this block is…
………………………………………………………………………………
………………………………………………………………………………

One thing I'd like to explore today is…
………………………………………………………………………………
………………………………………………………………………………

On first drafts: It is completely raw, the sort of thing I feel free to do with the door shut—it's the story undressed, standing up in nothing but its socks and undershorts.

— Stephen King

I FEEL TOO MUCH PRESSURE.

PROBLEM

> Putting too many expectations on yourself and your writing.

I know you want to write a brilliant book or essay, so you're holding yourself and your writing to a high standard. It's such a natural desire to produce the best quality work we can manage. But a strange thing can happen when we come to our writing with the intention to create a perfect or even a great draft. With this expectation, we often have trouble producing even a few simple sentences because the pressure is simply too much. We are actively sabotaging our own productivity by creating this pressure.

SOLUTION

> Let go of your expectations.

Before you start writing, you have to look for and drop as many unrealistic expectations you have put on yourself and your writing as possible. Start by reviewing your goals. Are you feeling overwhelmed and intimidated by them? If so, you can easily adjust your goals by reading the next chapter.

Right now, close your eyes, take a deep breath, and ask yourself if you can identify any expectations you have for yourself or your writing. Become a real detective and look for the invisible pressures! When you see them in your mind, write them down and intentionally let them go. Breathe them out completely for now, and for the next hour, allow yourself to approach your writing clear of any expectations. See what happens. After the hour is up, you can compare writing without expectations to writing under their pressure and see what you noticed.

In the present moment, there is no pressure. All you have to do is put down one word. And then another. And then two and three more. Hopefully, they make a sentence. Stay here, in this moment. With this sentence in front of you, and with this feeling inside you. Being relaxed, authentic, and present in the moment is all that's required. It will naturally create a writing flow.

When you are open, accepting, and curious about your process and your ideas, you will be much more productive. And don't get too attached to the words you write. It's okay to change your mind and cut them later, but for now, you have one simple task to accomplish. Just listen in and say one thing you feel is true for you in simple words. And then another. Later you can make your sentences more complex, but for now, try to relax all your expectations of yourself and your writing and see how fast and easy the words start flowing!

Relax, play, and enjoy every sentence. Allow yourself to be incorrect, to make mistakes, to try and fail. Allow yourself to learn, to grow, and to enjoy the process of discovery. Writing is a form of discovery, after all. Once you learn to trust it and experience even one moment of free flowing, passionate, and authentic writing, it can be your guiding star. And one day, this can become your daily writing experience.

PRACTICAL IDEAS TO TRY

Enjoy playing with these creative ideas to jumpstart your session!

- Ask yourself, "Why is this so hard?" and respond honestly by freewriting for five minutes.

- Imagine you have no audience. No supervisor, no publisher, no readers, and no critics. Write down three things you would write if you were only writing for yourself.

- What is the biggest pressure you feel right now? What does it look like? What does it say? Draw a cartoon of it and add speech bubbles with words you hear in your head.

- Freewrite for five minutes about what you would like your writing to feel like. What would a healthy relationship with your writing look like? How would you know if your relationship with your writing became great? What would that feel like?

PROMPTS

Finish the sentences below as quickly as you can, and as many times as you want. Afterwards, freewrite for five minutes about any responses that surprised you.

The biggest pressure I feel right now is to...
....
....

The biggest stress I feel right now is...
....
....

What I'm afraid to find out is...
....
....

If I didn't feel any pressure, I'd write about...
....
....

My writing should be...
....
....

I should be...
....
....

Abandon the idea that you are ever going to finish. Lose track of the 400 pages and write just one page for each day, it helps. Then when it gets finished, you are always surprised.

— John Steinbeck

I FEEL OVERWHELMED BY HOW MUCH I HAVE TO DO.

PROBLEM

> Your goals are not adapted for daily practice.

Having too high a goal can paralyze us and prevent us from taking a simple step. It's just too overwhelming. The problem is not you. And there's nothing wrong with your goals. It's just that your long term goals haven't been adapted for daily progress. The good news is this is very easy to adjust. I will show you how to articulate a long-term goal so you know exactly what to do each day, and at your own pace.

SOLUTION

> Adjust your long-term goals for daily progress.

There are two steps in creating an optimal goal-setting process. The first one is to check if your long-term goals are realistic and aligned with your natural writing pace.

For example, if you aim to write 240 pages in three months, let's divide the number of pages by the number of weeks available (12), and you have a weekly goal of 20 pages. If we divide the 20 pages by the number of workdays (5), we get a daily goal of four pages a day. I can hear you protesting that there are seven days in a week. Yes, and you must schedule one or two days off during the week.

Can you consistently produce four pages a day and feel no stress? If so, you're all set. I'd say that four pages is still too much to produce consistently every day for months. I would recommend setting your daily goals as low as possible at first so you can experience the magic of consistency and joy of accomplishment. Just commit to showing up and experiment with working in small sprints. It's enough for now.

Let's now move on to step two, where we reevaluate your long-term goal, using your natural pace.

Do you know your writing pace? How many pages do you usually write in a day?

Based on your natural pace, calculate how many pages you can realistically accomplish in the next week, month, or a year. Start by setting a goal in minutes and another in pages, for example, one hour or one page a day, whichever goal you reach first. If you can write one page in 10 minutes, then you're free for the day. No guilt. No unfinished goals. But if you can't seem to produce a page, then after one hour of trying, you've met your time-based goal and are also free for the day.

Even if you write only one page a day, by the end of one year, you'd have 365 pages, enough for a whole book! If you took 1-2 days off every week, you'd have a little less, but you get the point. I can see your shoulders drop and your whole body relax, because you no longer have to be overwhelmed by carrying your whole project in your head all day, every day. You can put it down and only focus on one page, march over to your desk and complete that goal in minutes, not hours. And you can walk away with confidence that if you do this for the scheduled five days each week, you are on your way to completing your long-term goal. No guesswork necessary. Congratulations!

PRACTICAL IDEAS TO TRY

Enjoy playing with these creative ideas to jumpstart your session!

- What would you like to accomplish in the next 12 months? How many pages will this contain?
  E.g. Let's say you'd like to write 260 pages.

- Break down your long-term goal into 52 weeks. What is your weekly goal in pages? Write it down.
  E.g. 260 pages divided by 52 weeks is five pages.

- If you write five out of seven days (I highly recommend scheduling two days off), how many pages do you have to produce each day? Write it down.
  E.g. Your daily goal is one page.

PROMPTS

Finish the sentences below as quickly as you can, and as many times as you want. Afterwards, freewrite for five minutes about any responses that surprised you.

My main focus in this paragraph is...
....
....

I feel overwhelmed by...
....
....

What I'd really like to say here is...
....
....

Right now I could write a page about...
....
....

The one thing I'd like to focus on for the next 10 minutes is...
....
....

We have to continually be jumping off cliffs and developing our wings on the way down.
— Kurt Vonnegut

I CAN'T START UNTIL I KNOW HOW IT'S ALL GOING TO FIT TOGETHER.

PROBLEM

> The need to know is the enemy of the flow.

We are programmed to fear the unknown. This fear helped us survive for thousands of years. However, while completely understandable, your need for certainty might be the very thing creating your writer's block. It's simply not possible to know in the beginning of the writing journey how it's all going to fit together in the end. Don't let this prevent you from writing. Instead, you can let writing teach you about uncertainty and stay open to the experience.

SOLUTION

> Let go of your need to know.

*T*ry not knowing and writing anyway. Try wondering and exploring instead. Don't expect everything to go to plan. Learn to trust the process and yourself. Allow your words and ideas the freedom to develop and change. Some things we can only find out by writing. Dive in. Jump without a parachute, and let your writing give you wings!

You're not carving things in stone. You're just typing out some words. If you don't like them later, you can delete them, but first you need to find your momentum. Without overthinking what's next, you will notice how much easier it becomes to express yourself, how authentic your voice is, and how fluid your writing becomes.

You can forget your whole book and stay with one idea at a time. One movement of your mind. Allow things to emerge, consider them, and if they don't resonate, let go of them next time you edit. In my book *Dissertation*

Without Tears, I call this method *writing in time*, and explain in detail how it differs from *writing in space*. Let me share a quick summary here.

Writing in space is trying to envision the complete picture of your future finished draft, holding all the pieces in your head, and trying to fit each new word into the structure you'd imagined. Writing in time is different. You start from the present moment and pull on each thought or feeling to discover the next, like you'd pull on a thread, sensing what idea this sentence naturally leads to. You move slowly and organically from one idea to another, following them and writing them down as they occur in your mind. You listen to each note in the piece you're composing. You give attention to every word, phrase, and chord, and slowly a melody emerges, creating a symphony of notes, words, and movements. This kind of writing is a discovery process that unfolds moment by moment, and it is very gentle to both the writer and the reader.

Writing in space can also be useful in its kinder form. Imagining what your work will look like can be energizing, but it's good to remember that it's only one possibility. The outline is not set in stone, so you can use a lighter, more playful way to discover the structure as you go. When outlining, you're looking for clarity, not pressure, nor feeling stuck in a certain structure.

PRACTICAL IDEAS TO TRY

Enjoy playing with these creative ideas to jumpstart your session!

- Write down three topics that you are curious to explore at the moment, even if you don't know yet how they'll fit into the big picture or if you will choose to explore them. These are just possible directions for your current project. Freewrite for five minutes about each. Does one of them have energy and connect easily with a specific part of your project?

- Take a large sheet of paper and draw symbols or images to represent the major parts of your project. Then, draw out the connections you see among them, making notes on how they could fit together. Repeat as needed.

- Put all major parts of your project onto sticky notes and place them on a wall or a door. Try organizing them in different patterns and take a photo of each. After you have had some distance from your work, look at these photos on your phone and reflect on one possible structure you're excited to try right now.

PROMPTS

Finish the sentences below as quickly as you can, and as many times as you want. Afterwards, freewrite for five minutes about any responses that surprised you.

One thing I'd love to explore right now is…
………………………………………………………………………………
………………………………………………………………………………

One thing that really draws me today is…
………………………………………………………………………………
………………………………………………………………………………

If I didn't need to know how it's all going to fit together, I would write about…
………………………………………………………………………………
………………………………………………………………………………

What would be quite easy to write about right now is…
………………………………………………………………………………
………………………………………………………………………………

The one thing I'd actually enjoy writing about is…
………………………………………………………………………………
………………………………………………………………………………

Planning to write is not writing. Outlining, researching, talking to people about what you're doing, none of that is writing. Writing is writing.
— E. L. Doctorow

I DON'T KNOW WHERE TO START.

PROBLEM

> Your focus is misplaced.

When you sit down to write, it's not the best time to start planning or organizing your writing tasks. The time for planning and organizing precedes writing time. Now your focus should be entirely on writing, and you should know exactly where you are starting today. When you start your writing session by planning, you are making your experience more challenging than it needs to be. You also increase the risk of creating a frustrating loop with writing and planning disrupting each other.

SOLUTION

> Separate writing and planning.

Planning and writing are so different that mixing them together practically guarantees that you won't achieve writing momentum. Our planning mind is future-oriented and requires a different focus. To plan efficiently, we have to create distance between ourselves and our project and take in the whole picture. In a way, our goal is to unfocus our gaze and see all parts of our project at once. Writing, on the other hand, is most successful when we achieve a single focus and are present with every word and movement of our thoughts and energy.

These two tasks need to be done at different times. I usually plan my next day's goal right after completing my writing goal for the day. In that moment, I feel happy and connected to my work, so my planning reflects that clarity and takes one minute to jot down a few ideas for tomorrow. I do it directly in the document, usually on the first page, so when I open my document the day after, I have a few specific goals I can start with. I call this method *parking downhill*.

You can plan weekly, daily, at the end of your writing session, or at any other time, but it has to be before your writing time. This way, when it's time to write, you know exactly where to start, and your focus can be exclusively on the task in front of you. Usually, what's in front of you is one idea, one sentence, or one word you need to put down on paper. Sounds manageable, doesn't it? Big exhale. To achieve that single focus, always start writing in the moment. The power of immediate action will surprise you. And it won't let your inner critic take you for another loop. If you need help breaking up with your inner critic, I share 58 specific ways in *Dissertation Without Tears*.

Set an immediate and ridiculously easy goal for the start of your writing session. For example, you can write down one sentence, or three keywords for the next section, or freewrite for three minutes about all the things you hate about this section. I'm not suggesting that you stop after completing that task. This is your warm up—to put you into an "I can do it" mindset. Once you accomplish a small goal, you will feel less resistant to write a bit more, and soon enough, instead of going in circles, you will be enjoying the writing flow.

PRACTICAL IDEAS TO TRY

Enjoy playing with these creative ideas to jumpstart your session!

- At the end of each session, jot down three ideas you'd like to continue developing in the next session. Perhaps you'd like to expand on a definition, find an example to illustrate a point, or find a more suitable metaphor for this section.

- From your list of ideas, pick one that speaks to you the most and set your alarm for five minutes. Until your alarm goes off, write down everything that comes to mind about this idea without stopping. Don't overthink it. Just write. Once your alarm goes off, get up and celebrate! You can now repeat this exercise with another idea. No pressure. No stress. Just one idea at a time.

- Write down three small goals you can accomplish in the next five minutes. E.g. open the file, rename it, highlight the two paragraphs you will focus on first, highlight the best part of your conclusion.

- Set your alarm for five minutes and write down all your thoughts and feelings about the current section.

PROMPTS

Finish the sentences below as quickly as you can, and as many times as you want. Afterwards, freewrite for five minutes about any responses that surprised you.

Right now I really want to write about…
…………………………………………………………………………………
…………………………………………………………………………………

The most important idea to express today is…
…………………………………………………………………………………
…………………………………………………………………………………

I still want to write about…
…………………………………………………………………………………
…………………………………………………………………………………

Right now I could easily write a paragraph about…
…………………………………………………………………………………
…………………………………………………………………………………

If I had to choose a metaphor for how I feel right now, it would be…
…………………………………………………………………………………
…………………………………………………………………………………

*Find your best time of the day
for writing and write.
Don't let anything else interfere.
Afterwards it won't matter
to you that the kitchen is a mess.
— Esther Freud*

I HAVE TOO MANY THINGS TO DO BEFORE I CAN START WRITING.

PROBLEM

> You have not prioritized your writing.

Writing takes time and attention. If you don't make an effort to prioritize your writing, you're setting yourself up for failure. You've probably noticed that many other things will gladly present as urgent and swallow your writing time whole. If, while sitting at your desk, instead of focusing on your writing, you are responding to emails or making a grocery list, you are contributing to an internal environment of frustration that will likely cause writer's block. The good news is this is easy to fix.

SOLUTION

> Prioritize your writing.

For your writing to flourish, it has to take up some of your time, energy, and focused attention on a regular basis. Trying to squeeze your writing in between existing schedules, appointments, and other commitments might be a costly mistake. You must schedule your writing sessions. And you must protect them with your life. So put them in your calendar and say NO to any requests that interfere with this protected time! You can emphasize your intention to honour these scheduled sessions by naming them something funny in your calendar, like "NO TRESPASSING," "UNTOUCHABLE," OR "WRITING NINJA

SPRINT" until you notice the difference they make in your productivity and start honouring them effortlessly.

The simple truth is, if you are serious about your writing goals, then you must prioritize them. Schedules will need to be examined and renegotiated if necessary, and some existing responsibilities will need to be cancelled or postponed. There comes a moment when you feel that precious momentum in your work. It's happening, coming together, and wants to be written. This is the moment to acknowledge to yourself that writing has become one of your main priorities for the next little while. You must share with the people closest to you that your mental and emotional availability will not be the same for a little bit, and that while you're finishing this project, you will need much more alone writing time.

It's better to share this with them, ask for their help, and tell them you will be a better parent, spouse, and friend once you finish your writing goals for the day. It's better to have this conversation than to become chronically frustrated that you are unable to write and accidentally snap at people you love.

The writing momentum takes a while to create, and it is your responsibility to safeguard it by giving your writing your time, attention, and energy. So be brave, ask your family for help, and remember to express appreciation for their support and the sacrifices they make.

PRACTICAL IDEAS TO TRY

Enjoy playing with these creative ideas to jumpstart your session!

- Schedule five short morning writing sessions in the next week and honour them. Try to schedule at least a 45-minute session each day. Learn to be with your writing the first thing in the morning before you attend to your daily chores.

- At the end of the week, journal for at least 15 minutes about what you noticed this week, and how your relationship with your project is changing.

- Set 10 small goals for this week and put them into your calendar, so you know what exactly you will be working on each day. Make them measurable and keep checking them off when done. Don't forget to celebrate each one, even if it's just an acknowledgement, a big delicious stretch, or a deep exhale. You can also go to the mirror and give yourself two thumbs up and a big smile. You deserve it!

PROMPTS

Finish the sentences below as quickly as you can, and as many times as you want. Afterwards, freewrite for five minutes about any responses that surprised you.

What I could easily do in the next 15 minutes is...
………………………………………………………………………………
………………………………………………………………………………

Three things I can do by the end of the hour are...
………………………………………………………………………………
………………………………………………………………………………

One thing in my calendar I could replace with a short writing session today is...
………………………………………………………………………………
………………………………………………………………………………

Tomorrow morning, I could write for 30-45 minutes before...
………………………………………………………………………………
………………………………………………………………………………

Today I can carve out 30 minutes for writing after...
………………………………………………………………………………
………………………………………………………………………………

Focus more on your desire than on your doubt, and the dream will take care of itself.
— Mark Twain

I HATE WRITING!

PROBLEM

> Not taking responsibility for creating a fulfilling writing experience.

Often the problem starts with the way we've defined our relationship with our writing and our project. Have you taken a moment to think about it? If you see your writing project as a monster who is only here to terrorize you, no wonder writing feels like torture. With thoughts like this, how can you possibly have fun or be passionate about your project? It's not your fault. It's only your thinking. You might've learned from your parents or teachers that writing is always hard. Now, your ideas about your writing are in your way, but you can easily change this!

SOLUTION

> Get curious about your process.

The fastest way to change your experience of writing is to become aware of your relationship with your writing. Do you have one? What's the status? Are you currently in a committed, loyal, joyous and fulfilling relationship? Or do you hate each other and come together because you are obligated to see each other until you finish this project?

What is your definition of writing? Can you look deeply and discover the flaws in it? Have you defined it as hard work, or even some sort of punishment? Let's change that and discover how to play more and work less while writing.

Instead of being militant about your discipline and pushing yourself to write when you don't want to, you can become curious about your writing process, get creative with it, and redefine it completely!

Do you feel joy or resentment when you approach your writing desk? How would you like to feel? How will you know when writing becomes enjoyable? Have you ever had this experience? What made it fun and joyful?

To encounter more joy, be prepared to let go of some of your attachments and ideas about writing. It can be eye-opening to challenge your own thinking. To help you discover things about your unique process, keep asking yourself: "Which part of my writing process is fun? What do I love the most about working on this project? What is working well for me, and what do I love about my writing time? What would bring me joy?"

For me, it's the act of discovery, self-honesty, letting go of control, listening to my heart, and letting my fingers write freely. It's also the sense of openness, a feeling of possibility and authentic self-expression, a sense of wholeness and courage. It's joy and freedom.

But you are unique. What I love doesn't matter or apply to your process. That's why it's crucial for you to find your own answers and insights. Here are some simple tools to help find out what works for you and what doesn't.

PRACTICAL IDEAS TO TRY

Enjoy playing with these creative ideas to jumpstart your session!

- Create two lists. In one, list all the things that make writing fun for you, and in the other one, list all the things that make it hard. Don't make it complicated. Just try to note 2-3 things for each column right now. Keep adding to your lists day after day, and keep this new research project going until you get some answers. When you find and acknowledge those small positive moments, try to intentionally create more of them in your practice!

- Text yourself throughout the day whenever you have a question or an idea about your current project. You can do this while waiting for an elevator or a bus.

- Go for a walk with a pen and a stack of sticky notes and plan out your next book, chapter, paper, article, blog. One idea at a time. One small idea per note.

- Jot down your ideas while in the shower. Just tape a piece of plastic to the wall and use a permanent marker to write on it.

PROMPTS

Finish the sentences below as quickly as you can, and as many times as you want. Afterwards, freewrite for five minutes about any responses that surprised you.

My relationship with my writing has been...
....
....

Writing used to be fun when I...
....
....

What would make writing fun for me today is...
....
....

What I'd like my writing process to feel like is...
....
....

My favourite part about writing is...
....
....

A professional writer is an amateur who didn't quit.
— Richard Bach

PART 2
I CAN'T CONTINUE!

You just have to go on when it is worst and most helpless—there is only one thing to do with a novel and that is go straight on through to the end of the damn thing.

— *Ernest Hemingway*

I'M STUCK IN THIS SECTION AND CAN'T MOVE ON UNTIL I FIGURE IT OUT.

PROBLEM

> Staying in one spot for too long.

You know how exhilarating writing momentum can be! You might also know that inertia has its own momentum, too. It feels heavier and more sticky with every moment it continues. If you're stuck in one section for too long, your mind will start playing tricks on you, suggesting catastrophic conclusions like, "I can't write," "This will never work," etc. The longer you keep spinning your wheels, the harder it is to get unstuck. Your inner critic pounces on those moments of self-doubt and, if you're not careful, can turn them into days and weeks.

SOLUTION

(Move on!)

There are a couple of ways to do this when you feel the momentum slowing down. One of the easiest ways is to set a 3-day writing ban on the section you're struggling with and switch to another section. And it doesn't have to be the next one. You can choose what to write based on where your interest is right now. The point is to not stay stuck for more than a few minutes, and to let go of the rigid idea of a linear writing process. Flexibility will create progress. Rigidity will likely stifle it.

There's another trick that works miracles! When you feel stuck, instead of writing about your topic, switch to writing about your frustration. Don't just think about it—for this to work, you have to do it in writing. Explore why this particular section is so challenging for you. Ask questions of yourself and your document. Write about what you're feeling. Dump it all onto the page. Often, all you need is five minutes of freewriting before you're ready to move back to your main task. Sometimes even less. Since most of the obstacles are emotional and psychological, the clarity you achieve might help your writing to flow with ease for the rest of the day. I highly recommend it!

The point is to write *through* the interference, so you can quickly regain writing momentum with new clarity on what the block was really about. You will feel lighter and more clear. About the task at hand, about your process, and about your capacity to move through writing blocks in the future.

And the good news is—not only did you avoid writer's block, but you also prevented your inner critic from bullying you with ideas about your writing capacity. It's time to celebrate because you have discovered for yourself that becoming a victim of your inner critic and getting stuck for weeks are both optional. I'm proud of you! Congratulations!

PRACTICAL IDEAS TO TRY

Enjoy playing with these creative ideas to jumpstart your session!

- Write about what you're struggling with in this section. E.g., "I feel like I'm not very clear when I describe X." You can do this in a journal, in the margins, or directly in the document—just change the font colour to separate it from the main text.

- Ask a friend, a colleague, or your partner for 5-10 minutes of their time. Take a minute to tell them about the section in which you are stuck, and invite them to ask you questions about what they've heard and to share what they've noticed.

- Go for a walk and have an imaginary chat with a friend about this section. Tell them the struggle, ask questions on their behalf, and respond to them.

- Set the alarm for five minutes, and jot down 10 possible directions for this section, no matter how feasible they seem. Freewrite about anything that comes up in response to the list. Does one direction feel more inviting than the rest?

PROMPTS

Finish the sentences below as quickly as you can, and as many times as you want. Afterwards, freewrite for five minutes about any responses that surprised you.

One potential direction this section could go in is...
....
....

It feels most natural to connect this section to...
....
....

If this section was a movie, the next scene could look like...
....
....

I feel this section is hard for me because...
....
....

The hardest part about this section is that I don't know...
....
....

*In nature, nothing is perfect.
Trees can be contorted,
bent in weird ways and
they're still beautiful.*
— *Alice Walker*

I'VE REWRITTEN THIS SECTION FIVE TIMES, BUT CAN'T MOVE ON UNTIL IT'S POLISHED.

PROBLEM

> You're combining writing and editing.

Your feeling that the section is not perfect is valid. It needs more polishing—it's true. You have the discernment to know that and naturally you want to make it better. However, thinking you need to stay with this section until it's perfect before moving on is counterproductive. It's just a case of good old perfectionism trying to sabotage your momentum. I'm afraid you're about to commit the worst writing crime—combining writing and editing. You're not alone. We all do this until we learn it doesn't work.

SOLUTION

(Separate writing and editing.)

*E*very writer dreams of writing momentum. Once you discover this flow, writing without it will seem like torture in comparison. You can't create it artificially, but you can set up the best potential conditions for it to manifest. The biggest mistake is introducing another activity—like editing—into your writing flow, because it will interrupt it.

Writing and editing are two completely different activities. Writing is dynamic and requires trust, acceptance, and momentum. Editing is more static and requires stillness, discernment, precision, patience, and grit.

To achieve the flow, focus on the act of writing in the here and now. Give yourself the gift of a single focus—

putting words on paper. If you can only spare 20 minutes, make them count. For those 20 minutes, you have to be focused on one thing and one thing only—writing! Not planning, nor outlining, nor revising, nor editing, nor proofreading. Writing. So, set the alarm and turn off the world for 20 minutes, or whatever your magic length of time is, and go full power!

Stay with your writing for as long as you feel the flow. Keep moving that pen and those fingers. Whatever you do, do not break the writing momentum. So leave your phone and your perfectionism in another room, enter the sacred temple of your creativity, close the door, and write your heart out!

To avoid worrying about the quality of your draft as you're writing, schedule your revisions in advance. Schedule 2-3 revision sessions for the following week, so you know that you have allowed ample time to look critically at your first draft. You will have enough time to go over your entire draft, read through it, check for cohesion, look at your points, structure, tone, word choice, etc.—just not at the same time as you're trying to write it. Because that is a trap.

Your only task in this moment is expressing yourself with authenticity. Enjoy this special moment of writing without your inner editor. I hope you love it!

PRACTICAL IDEAS TO TRY

Enjoy playing with these creative ideas to jumpstart your session!

- List three secret reasons you might be feeling anxious about finishing this chapter and sharing it with your readers.

- If you're writing down an idea and suddenly another idea comes—for fixing this section, restructuring it, or making it better—jot it down quickly and return to writing about your current idea or your paragraph. Don't switch your focus to the new idea before finishing the one before you.

- If in the middle of writing, you remembered a specific quote that would make this point better, do not go searching the Internet for it. Write down, "Quote about … " and keep writing.

- When you catch yourself slipping into an old habit of editing as you write, cover the page with a piece of paper if you're handwriting, or set your font colour to white if you're typing so you can't see and judge your words.

PROMPTS

Finish the sentences below as quickly as you can, and as many times as you want. Afterwards, freewrite for five minutes about any responses that surprised you.

If this section were complete, I would want to write about...
....
....

What I'm really worried about when it comes to this section...
....
....

I'm still unsure if...
....
....

What I'm clear about is...
....
....

What I'm really trying to say here is...
....
....

You never have to change anything you got up in the middle of the night to write.

— *Saul Bellow*

I'M GOING IN CIRCLES. I DON'T KNOW WHAT TO SAY.

PROBLEM

> You're not *that* interested in your subject.

You're either writing about something that's not important to you, or you're *not* writing about something that's important to you. That's your boulder. And you're trying to write around it.

It might feel impractical to switch to a new topic in the middle of a project. You might be afraid to disappoint someone or waste your previous effort. Whatever the reason, deep down you know that what you're doing is not authentic to you anymore. It was at one point, but now it's changed. And the sooner you acknowledge it, the easier your journey will become.

SOLUTION

> Stop trying to write around
> the boulder. Move it!

*E*ven if you convince yourself to stay the course against your intuition, write a few paragraphs around the boulder, and postpone the problem, you can be sure to expect another writer's block just down the road. The point is you can't write around the boulder forever! It's right there in the middle of your path, and it's stopping you from moving forward.

If, instead of postponing the problem, you find the strength to deal with the boulder and move it out of the way, you will create a new space where the boulder used to be. Then the stream of writing can go through the river bed and not around the boulder. You will create movement, flow, and, inevitably, the coveted writing momentum.

One way to create this movement and flow is to refocus on what matters to you the most and say what you really want to say simply and directly. When you find yourself fumbling through a specific paragraph, one quick trick you can try is to stop writing, take a deep breath, and draw a bold line under what you've just written. Use the speed, the pressure, and the energy of your hand to intentionally create a reset! Now write down, "What I'm *really* trying to say is…" and continue with the first thing that comes to you. This will help you refocus, get rid of clutter, and return to your core message!

You can also journal about the boulder, analyze it, talk to a friend or a counsellor about it, meditate on it, but you must face it and acknowledge its presence and impact on your writing. You can even look underneath the boulder for the hidden fears that keep you from moving it because you're afraid of what will surface. Try journaling about the reasons you're writing someone else's words and in someone else's voice. What prevents you from saying what you see and believe? You are the only one who can find out. Get curious about your internal obstacles.

I really hope that the practical strategies and prompts below will help you face and move the boulder from your path, even if it's difficult. A writing warrior like you can do courageous things like this. I believe in you!

PRACTICAL IDEAS TO TRY

Enjoy playing with these creative ideas to jumpstart your session!

- Imagine that you have completed your current project. It's sent, published, or printed. You've celebrated your accomplishment and now have to choose a completely new subject. Which three topics would you like to explore now? What did you notice as you were doing this exercise?
- Close your eyes and visualize sitting in front of the boulder blocking your path. There's just the two of you and no one else around for miles. Ask the boulder why it's not letting you pass. What's the precise action it wants you to take? What would it feel like to take it? Freewrite for five minutes.
- List 10 of your greatest writing fears right now. Quickly, without much thought, just list them using brief and incomplete phrases. Leave the list alone for a few hours or until the next day. When you come back, respond to each fear in freewriting. What have you noticed?
- Set your alarm for five minutes and write down three main points for the current section. Use short sentences. Set your alarm for five more minutes and write down three short sentences supporting each of the three points.

PROMPTS

Finish the sentences below as quickly as you can, and as many times as you want. Afterwards, freewrite for five minutes about any responses that surprised you.

I really don't want to write about... because...
....
....

I'm writing this section because...
....
....

What I'd really love to say is...
....
....

What I'd really love to explore right now is...
....
....

What I'm really curious about is...
....
....

*When I dare to be powerful,
to use my strength in
the service of my vision,
then it becomes less and less
important whether I am afraid.*
— Audre Lorde

I'M AFRAID OF BEING WRONG.

PROBLEM

> Focusing on being sure.

I've felt this fear in my own writing big time. I used to be deadly afraid to make mistakes. This kept me from trying things out and learning from trial and error. It also kept me from writing for weeks. Now I see that even though my desire to be correct was futile, it was necessary, if only to see how spinning my wheels won't give me any guarantees. We can worry about being correct forever, but we will never know for sure until we put our writing out there. Making mistakes is one of the most reliable ways to find out if our idea is correct. Someone will point out what we've overlooked, and we'll be able to see it! Effortlessly.

SOLUTION

> Be brave!

If you want to avoid writer's block forever, make expressing your truth in this moment your only goal. Accept the very real fear of making mistakes, but don't let it paralyze or silence you. You can develop a tolerance for the discomfort of uncertainty. You can give yourself permission to not know every answer, to explore, play, and have fun. Allow yourself to accept any outcome, including being completely wrong, and trust that you can deal with it. You'll have time in the future to revise, fact-check, and peer-review. But the real possibility for a breakthrough is this—in the face of uncertainty, you can learn to lean on self-trust instead of self-doubt!

This takes courage. But you already have it inside you! Let's look at two worst-case scenarios you have to choose from. If your worst fear comes true, and you find out you were wrong, you will simply make a correction and continue to enjoy your writing and exploring journey. The other worst-case scenario is you will remain stuck in the fear of making a mistake, and will continue to silently write in a perpetual state of stress and anxiety, or maybe you'll stop writing altogether. Each of us has to choose between these two options.

Writing is the perfect medium for exploration. If you trust it, it will show you your power to discern and allow you to build your self-trust. You can figure out if a direction is right for you by actually writing about it and paying close attention to how you feel. Does your idea feel right in this moment? Then you have to be brave, share what you see and believe, and be willing to be completely and utterly wrong.

This is a gift to yourself and a great remedy against writer's block—to allow yourself to write with no pressure to be correct before you even had a chance to explore. I hope you allow yourself to trust your writing practice and your intuition more and more each day. When you feel the fear of making a mistake, you can lean on these two questions: Can you bear the thought of being wrong and allow yourself to write? Will you allow yourself to express what you feel, think, and see as true in this moment?

PRACTICAL IDEAS TO TRY

Enjoy playing with these creative ideas to jumpstart your session!

- Set your timer for five minutes and start writing about something that you want to clarify for yourself. Freewrite with no expectation to discover the one correct answer. Try out any answer that seems plausible. Take a break.

- Now read what you've written. Do you see something that doesn't fit, is confusing, or incomplete? Take a step back, and freewrite about another solution, answer, or interpretation by setting the alarm for another five minutes. You are only trying and exploring. You are not required by law to laminate your draft. Or even show it to anyone. It's safe to try.

- If you knew you couldn't fail in your thinking, conclusions, or a direction you want to take your writing, what would you really love to write about? Is there anything you're dying to express, regardless of being right or wrong? Can you give yourself permission to just write it out?

PROMPTS

Finish the sentences below as quickly as you can, and as many times as you want. Afterwards, freewrite for five minutes about any responses that surprised you.

If I weren't worried about being wrong, I'd write about…

……………………………………………………………………………

……………………………………………………………………………

In this moment, my intuition tells me that the best direction to follow is…

……………………………………………………………………………

……………………………………………………………………………

I'm afraid to make a mistake because I'm afraid to be seen as…

……………………………………………………………………………

……………………………………………………………………………

I must never make mistakes because…

……………………………………………………………………………

……………………………………………………………………………

What I'm afraid to explore is…

……………………………………………………………………………

……………………………………………………………………………

We delight in the beauty of the butterfly, but rarely admit the changes it has gone through to achieve that beauty.
— *Maya Angelou*

NOTHING IS GOING TO PLAN! MIGHT AS WELL GIVE UP.

PROBLEM

> Expecting your writing process to go according to plan.

*E*very writer wants their writing to follow their plan. Unfortunately, this is not a reality. It's okay to have this desire, but it's important to know that it's just a desire, and right now you have a choice—to feel helpless because the reality did not meet your expectation, or to embrace the reality and choose an effective action that's clear and true for you right now. Expecting your writing process to be smooth and predictable is the real problem. Luckily, it's up to you to drop that expectation.

SOLUTION

> Embrace the mess!

We make plans with the best of intentions. Plans are necessary and useful in helping us organize our work and ideas. But we also need to build a tolerance for when our writing doesn't follow our plan or meet our expectations. Make a plan. Set goals. And then... let them go. Be patient. Accept the inevitable detours of the writing process. Be ready for them in advance. Let self-compassion be your guide.

An experienced writer knows that the creative journey has both ups and downs, and all you can do is be open, ready, and welcoming. Trust that when the wave goes down, you will be creative, resourceful, and resilient enough to intuit the right solution in the moment.

You have the capacity to embrace every stage of the writing process. Have faith that sometimes going in circles in the dark is necessary. Stay with your circles, with your ideas, and with your writer within, let go of your expectations, and lean on patience and trust. Take a break if you need to, support yourself, acknowledge your limitations, and trust your writing process. Know that it's the darkest before dawn, and a breakthrough will emerge.

You don't need to remain stuck in your old plan. If it's not working in this moment, it's not a disaster or a failure. It means your discernment is growing, and you can see what you couldn't see before. You are wiser than you were before. I mean it.

You don't have to completely throw away your old plan either. You can use it to find a new direction. Look at what upset you the most when things did not go according to plan. What did you feel could be lost? If it's still important to you, how can you integrate it into your new plan?

When you remember your *why* and remind yourself what's at stake, you will be able to persevere in the face of fallen plans, unmet expectations, and seeming failures. You will allow yourself to develop a new perspective and try another approach. Each moment is a fresh start. Including this one. But for you to persevere and refocus, you have to remain kind to yourself and your writing after your original plan fails. You have already made a breakthrough by understanding your process better and putting down some of your old expectations. Congratulations!

PRACTICAL IDEAS TO TRY

Enjoy playing with these creative ideas to jumpstart your session!

- Create a new file and call it Draft Ideas or Messy Words. Name it something that intentionally signals "imperfect." Give yourself permission to play and freewrite. Put some words on paper. Write about your project. Write why it's important. Just start anywhere because guess what, writing has a momentum, and once you start, you're *already* in the writing mode.
- Allow yourself five minutes to explore three possible directions for the section you're working on. Freewrite by hand. Don't show it to anyone. Just try to notice, in this moment, which direction feels true and which doesn't.
- Go for a walk and record your new, fragile, unformed ideas by talking about them out loud into your phone.
- Look for a new direction in nature. Go for a walk and closely observe things around you. Look at every tree, bush, leaf, branch, stone and bird you come across. Look at a stream if you have one nearby. Notice and be inspired by the organic patterns. Find something that resonates with a new direction you feel at the moment and write about it.

PROMPTS

Finish the sentences below as quickly as you can, and as many times as you want. Afterwards, freewrite for five minutes about any responses that surprised you.

If I gave up my old plan, I would love to explore...
....
....

If I never have to show this draft to anyone, right now I'd love to write about...
....
....

My inner critic says that I should write about...
....
....

What wants to be written right now is...
....
....

I'm inspired to write about...
....
....

*Take rest; a field
that has rested gives a
bountiful crop.*

—*Ovid*

I'M TOO TIRED TO CONTINUE WRITING.

PROBLEM

> You've been working too long without a break.

It seems logical that taking a break would only make your writer's block last longer. After all, I'm asking you to step away from your work. This seems counterintuitive, and I understand the impulse to write as much as possible without a break, even if it means staring at the screen, unable to write another sentence. If you are pushing yourself while feeling exhausted and overwhelmed, your writing will show it.

The quality of your writing depends on the clarity of your seeing. It depends on the quality of your attention, your ability to focus, and the amount of space in you available for insight.

SOLUTION

> Commit to a healthy and sustainable process.

One of the hardest tasks I face in my writing retreats is making my hardworking writers take a break. Here's what happens. When they come to their first retreat, they often try to work for 12 hours straight. As a result, they get burnt out and sabotage their own progress. They also ask me why I keep telling them to leave the stuffy room and take a break outside—they've come to work, after all. Even our private beach and island park can't help me convince them. Unless I threaten to roll their chairs outside onto the lawn, they stay glued to their screens.

The second time they come to the retreat, they take frequent breaks like clockwork, they exceed their goals, and when they leave on Friday, after a super productive week, they still feel fresh and energized, ready to continue their momentum into the weekend. They know. They tell others. There is a question in their feedback form, "What would you say to someone considering this retreat?" And they consistently respond, "Listen to Natalya and take breaks outside as often as you can!" Now they know what works and what doesn't!

Renewing your energy, maintaining your clarity of mind, and refreshing your focus with frequent breaks will allow you to meet your goals and enjoy every step of the process.

Rest, fresh air, movement, and reflection time will help you reach your goals faster. It's best to schedule a few breaks throughout your work period instead of crashing at the end of a 10-hour writing marathon and taking a week to recover. So when you're beginning to feel tired, get up and rest until you feel restored. Go for a walk, do a workout, or close your eyes and meditate. Your energy is a renewable resource. You can reset it at any moment. If you allow yourself such luxury and such deep wisdom, that is.

Please know that a healthy and sustainable writing practice is multi-dimensional, and every dimension is equally important. It includes a balance of working and resting, resetting, renewing, and reflecting as often as possible, and enjoying the resulting clarity and productivity.

PRACTICAL IDEAS TO TRY

Enjoy playing with these creative ideas to jumpstart your session!

- Surround yourself with comfy pillows and write in bed. If it's warm, go outside and write in the park or by the water, on the grass, or on a swing. Change the setting to reset your energy.

- Schedule a 15-minute break after every 200 words, or a 30-minute break after every 400 words—find the right combination for you. Do anything you like for 15 minutes—take a nap, do some stretching, watch part of your favourite show, take a shower, or do a mini-workout. But at the end of your scheduled break, come back for another sprint.

- Schedule three 30-minute writing sprints in the morning and rest in the afternoon and evening. Do not come back to your writing until the following day. Do this for a week. What have you noticed? Have you produced more or fewer words than usual?

- Write for 15 minutes out of every hour and rest for 45 minutes. I can see your shock, but this one was one of my best writing strategies in the last year of my PhD. It. Just. Works.

PROMPTS

Finish the sentences below as quickly as you can, and as many times as you want. Afterwards, freewrite for five minutes about any responses that surprised you.

After the next 200 words, I will take a break and enjoy...

....

....

After my three sprint sessions, I will enjoy... for the rest of the day!

....

....

My reward for meeting my goal today will be...

....

....

I look forward to... during my two full days off this week.

....

....

Find out the reason that commands you to write; see whether it has spread its roots into the very depth of your heart; confess to yourself you would have to die if you were forbidden to write.
— Rainer Maria Rilke

I DON'T FEEL LIKE WRITING TODAY. OR EVER. I QUIT!

PROBLEM

> You've lost connection with your purpose.

A writing process is rarely all smooth sailing. There will be days when you just don't feel like crawling out of bed to your desk. The first thing you need to realize is that there is absolutely nothing wrong with having a day like this. In fact, it's normal. Your inspiration is not gone forever. You're not a bad writer. Your writing dreams are not over. You're just having a low moment of self-doubt.

It's important to keep yourself from spiralling further when you feel insecure. It's best to be prepared for days like this and stay grounded in knowing that there are tools and strategies you can use to jumpstart your writing. Be there to support yourself in these moments.

SOLUTION

> Reconnect with your *Why*.

First of all, a breakdown can be productive. Honesty is a great gift. You know something is not working. You don't know why yet, but your feelings are loud and clear. Slow down and allow yourself a few minutes to acknowledge what you're feeling in full, knowing that this is temporary. You can journal for five minutes and ask yourself questions about the block and answer them honestly. It's for your eyes only.

Now it's time to reset your energy. Go for a run, a walk, take a shower, dance to your favourite song, or listen to it with your eyes closed, do a short yoga session, or meditate. Whatever it takes to get you out of this energy you've been feeling. Now that you've reset, it's time to get motivated and reconnect with your *Why*.

Remember the moment you first thought of starting your current project. Why did you want to do it? What inspired you and started the fire? What would it mean to you to finish it and to share it with the world? You can also turn to your favourite authors who inspired you to start writing in the first place. Embrace their advice, read a page from their book or biography, or look at their quotes about writing or living your purpose. Do whatever you need to reset and get your inspiration back!

Another great tool to boost your motivation is a goal primer, which is just a visual or sensory cue that helps you imagine what it would feel like when you achieve your goal. Take a moment to think of a picture, an object, a sound, a smell, or a combination of these that come to mind when you imagine the moment you've reached your long-term goal. It can be a photo of someone who has achieved a similar goal, like a famous author with a motivational quote encouraging you to persevere. It can be a photo of someone with a published book in their hand, or someone crossing the stage in their PhD hood, or even someone crossing the finish line in a marathon. It can be a pebble from a beach to remind you of a vacation you will take once you finish the project.

Primers are proven to be very effective in helping to achieve long-term goals because they make it easier to activate goal-related behaviour. So, consider displaying it in your workspace as you're planning, drafting, or revising.

Finally, a reward system can also help skyrocket your motivation. So plan a small reward for the end of each goal or each work period. It can be a massage, a movie, a workout, a walk in nature, or a chat with a good friend. Schedule a phone date, put your running shoes by the desk—you get the idea!

PRACTICAL IDEAS TO TRY

Enjoy playing with these creative ideas to jumpstart your session!

- Before you start writing, spend five minutes preparing a reward for meeting today's goal, so you know that at the end of your productive day, you can enjoy it.

- Look at different art forms—paintings, sculptures, architectural marvels, photographs, etc. You can listen to classical music, opera, or a soundtrack to your favourite movie. When you feel inspired, run to your notebook or your computer and let the creative sparks fly!

- If you don't have one already, create a goal primer for yourself. Draw it, make a collage, or find an image online to print out and display in your workspace.

PROMPTS

Finish the sentences below as quickly as you can, and as many times as you want. Afterwards, freewrite for five minutes about any responses that surprised you.

What I wanted my project to do when I first started was...
....
....

My original vision for my project used to be...
....
....

My current vision for my project is...
....
....

My bigger intention is to...
....
....

It would make me really happy if I could help...
....
....

You must be unintimidated by your own thoughts because if you write with someone looking over your shoulder, you'll never write.
— *Nikki Giovanni*

WHAT I'M UNDERTAKING FEELS IMPOSSIBLE. I FEEL TOO DISCOURAGED TO CONTINUE.

PROBLEM

> You're trusting the wrong voice.

It's not uncommon to feel beaten down by your inner critic. Every writer has moments when their inner critic gets too loud, their dreams seem too far away, and they are facing a choice—to quit and walk away, or find the strength and a reason to persevere.

Have you ever asked yourself why you trust this voice so much? Why do you give it so much importance? Has it earned your trust or helped you in any way? What is your relationship with this voice?

SOLUTION

> Trust your writer within.

The funny part is you have never consciously entered into a relationship with your inner critic. At some point in your life, you just noticed the presence of this harsh voice in your head and innocently trusted it. So, in a way, you got tricked into a relationship that you don't remember choosing. It happens to all of us. Let me ask you something. Why are you staying in a relationship that's not working? Your freedom's at stake.

You have two different relationships to choose from. One is guaranteed to bring you down and rob you of any energy or enthusiasm you might have felt when you first imagined the project you're working on. This relationship is mentally, emotionally, or verbally abusive. If you nourish it, it will make you quit and walk away from your dreams.

The other relationship is nourishing for your writer's soul. It's supportive and gentle, passionate and exciting, and it will lift you up and carry you through all the ups and downs to the finish line!

The good news is you are the one who gets to choose which relationship you want to nourish. Now that you have seen that this voice is not reliable, kind, or helpful, you can choose to simply ignore it.

You can choose the other relationship—that with your gentle, open, vulnerable, and infinitely patient writer within! Do you have a relationship with them? Would you like to? How could you get to know each other better?

You can start by asking what your inner writer needs from you. What makes them happy? Start spending some time together every day. Can you feel how warm and welcoming their presence feels, how kind and encouraging their voice is?

I am so excited for you! Because once you discover and commit to this relationship, the sky's the limit! This is one of the best relationships in your life! I can't wait for the two of you to fall madly in love with each other and live happily ever after.

PRACTICAL IDEAS TO TRY

Enjoy playing with these creative ideas to jumpstart your session!

- If you hear your inner critic's comments as you're trying to write, jot them down on a separate piece of paper. Make a list of all the things your inner critic says. Keep listing them over a few weeks until you reach a point of saturation. If the same comment comes up more than once, make a note next to it on the list, so you can see which comments are most persistent. You might be surprised to find just a few stories playing on repeat.

- After you finish making the list of your inner critic's most persistent stories, write a response to the most stubborn belief. You can repeat this exercise with other beliefs, giving each response about five minutes of your time. What have you noticed?

- Tune into your writer within and ask them, "Dear (your name), what do you need?" Become still and try to hear what your writer within wants to say to you after all these years and write down their answer.

PROMPTS

Finish the sentences below as quickly as you can, and as many times as you want. Afterwards, freewrite for five minutes about any responses that surprised you.

My inner critic calls me…
……………………………………………………………………………
……………………………………………………………………………

If I didn't believe my inner critic, I would…
……………………………………………………………………………
……………………………………………………………………………

If I fell in love with my writer within, I could…
……………………………………………………………………………
……………………………………………………………………………

I first met my inner critic when I was…
……………………………………………………………………………
……………………………………………………………………………

My writer within is…
……………………………………………………………………………
……………………………………………………………………………

A Note from the Author

Thank you for reading this book. Creating a genuine connection with readers like you is why I wrote it. Thank you for your trust. I hope these ideas and prompts serve you as well as they served me. If after you've tried these, you have any questions or feedback, I'd love to hear from you. Feel free to email me directly at natalya@writingdissertationcoach.com

If you enjoyed the book, I'd appreciate a rating or a short review on Amazon or Goodreads. For an indie author, every review is a precious gift!

If you've been struggling with your inner critic, you can download seven FREE chapters from *Dissertation Without Tears: How to Break Up with Your Inner Critic and Nourish the Writer Within*, which dispels 58 common writing myths, at www.writingdissertationcoach.com/free

There you'll also find other FREE resources, including simple seven-minute writing meditations that will help you build an effective daily practice. For unique coaching programs and writing retreats, visit www.writingdissertationcoach.com

And when you're ready to break up with your inner critic and trade stress and overwhelm for clarity and joy, book a FREE call with me!

Let's make your writing dreams a reality!

www.ingramcontent.com/pod-product-compliance
Lightning Source LLC
Chambersburg PA
CBHW071401080526
44587CB00017B/3152